Written and Illustrated by Caroline Arnold

A Day and Night in the SONORAN DESERT

raintree
a Capstone company — publishers for children

Tap-tap, tap-tap! Tap-tap, tap-tap!

It is an early spring morning in the Sonoran Desert. A woodpecker drills a hole in a saguaro cactus. The tall plant will be a good place to build a nest. On the ground below, a coyote looks for a shady place to rest.

A saguaro cactus can grow up to 12–18 metres tall. It is the tallest type of cactus in the United States.

A hare spots the coyote and bounds away on long, strong legs.

3

A lizard warms its scaly body in the morning sun.
Near by, a hummingbird whirs its wings and sips
nectar. Its long bill fits the flower perfectly. High
on the rocky slopes, bighorn sheep nibble grass.

A hungry Gila monster comes out of its burrow. It looks for nests containing eggs or small animals to eat. The Gila monster kills its prey with a venomous bite.

A Gila monster can survive without food for up to one year by living on fat stored in its tail.

Shadows are short in the midday sun. Heat bakes the desert floor. *Coo, coo!* calls a roadrunner. It races after a small lizard and catches it in its bill. The roadrunner runs back to its nest to feed its young.

A desert tortoise searches for flowers, leaves and grasses. Its hard shell helps to keep it cool. The tortoise breaks off plants with its mouth and chews them. When the tortoise has finished eating, it goes back to its cool burrow.

A desert tortoise gets almost all of the water it needs from its food. It can live without drinking anything for up to one year.

By the afternoon the desert air is very hot. Most animals stay out of the sun. But the antelope ground squirrel does not seem to mind. It scampers across the desert floor, gathering seeds, fruit and insects. Its tail shades its body like an umbrella.

The squirrel keeps a lookout for snakes and other predators. A red-tailed hawk circles in the sky. It is looking for something to eat. The squirrel sees the hawk and dashes to safety inside its burrow.

Antelope ground squirrels often climb barrel cacti to eat the fruit. No one knows how they avoid getting stuck in the cacti's sharp spines.

Daylight fades and the desert air cools quickly. Night-time animals come out to hunt and feed. Peccaries grunt to one another as they search for roots, fruit and seeds. They use their noses like shovels to dig up cactus roots and other plants.

Peccaries are also called javelinas. They live in groups, sometimes of more than 20 animals.

A prickly pear cactus hides the entrance to a pack rat den. Its sharp thorns help to protect the pack rats from predators. Its ripe fruit is a good source of food, too. Pack rats collect seeds, leaves, cactus pads and spines, and store them in their den.

Stars twinkle in the clear desert sky. A ringtail climbs a cactus, looking for ripe fruit. Mice come out of their holes to collect seeds. A rattlesnake slips out from under a rock and gets ready to hunt. It can feel the ground vibrate when the mice move.

Whoo! Whoo! calls an owl. It searches on silent wings for rats, mice and other small animals. It catches them with its sharp talons. The owl carries its prey back to its nest.

A rattlesnake injects venom into its prey through hollow, pointed teeth called fangs.

13

MIDNIGHT

The cool midnight air is full of life. Bats swoop in the dark sky. Some chase tiny insects. Others drink nectar from cactus flowers.

A watering hole in the desert is called an oasis.

A-roo! A-roo! howls a coyote. All night long it hunts for food. It will eat insects, lizards, mice, fruit or whatever it can find. When the coyote finds a watering hole, it stops for a drink. Scorpions and tarantulas crawl near by, looking for spiders and insects to eat.

15

All through the night, desert animals are busy looking for food. A kangaroo rat finds some seeds and stuffs them into pouches in its cheeks. It will store the seeds in its burrow.

A kangaroo rat has long hind legs.
It can leap almost one metre in a single hop.

A kit fox looks and listens for rats and mice. Its large ears can hear their tiny, high-pitched sounds. The kit fox sees a kangaroo rat and pounces. But just in time, the kangaroo rat leaps away to safety.

The sky begins to get light, and the sun peeks over the horizon. Night-time animals settle down for the day. Owls return to their nests, the kit fox goes to its burrow and the peccaries curl up for a nap. It is time for day-time animals to wake up and start a new day. Lizards warm themselves, hares find leaves to nibble and birds collect food for their young.

Every day and every night, animals find food, water and safe places to rest in the desert. It provides them with everything they need.

What is a desert?

A desert is a dry place. It gets less than 25 centimetres of rain a year. There are four major deserts in North America: the Great Basin, the Mojave, the Chihuahuan and the Sonoran.

The Sonoran Desert covers parts of Arizona, California and the Mexican states of Baja California and Sonora. In summer, day-time temperatures can be more than 43 degrees Celsius. In winter, night-time temperatures can drop below freezing. Plants and animals that live in the Sonoran Desert have adapted to its extreme climate.

Throughout the day and night, animals are busy in the desert. Diurnal animals are active during the day. Nocturnal animals are active at night. Which animals in this book are diurnal? Which are nocturnal? Where do they live in the desert?

Where can you find deserts?

Deserts are found all over the world. Some are hot. Others are cold. The largest desert in the world is the Sahara Desert, in Africa. It covers more than 7.8 million square kilometres. Only about one-fifth of the world's deserts are sandy. Most deserts are rocky or mountainous.

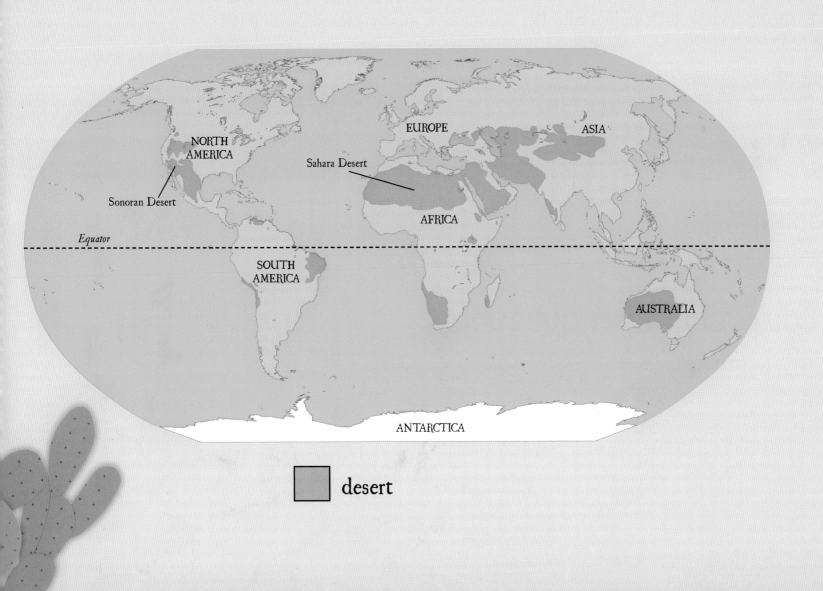

NORTH
AMERICA

Sonoran Desert

EUROPE   ASIA

Sahara Desert

AFRICA

Equator

SOUTH
AMERICA

AUSTRALIA

ANTARCTICA

☐ desert

Fun Facts

- A hare's large ears help it to keep cool. Blood flowing through the ears allows extra body heat to pass into the outside air.

- The Gila monster is the only venomous lizard in the United States. Its bright colours warn predators to stay away.

- Thick coats protect bighorn sheep from the hot desert sun during the day. They keep the sheep warm at night.

- Desert tortoises dig shallow holes in the ground. When it rains, the holes fill with water for the tortoises to drink.

- A roadrunner does not usually fly, but it is a speedy runner. It can run up to 32 kilometres an hour as it chases prey.

- When peccaries sense danger, they cough loudly and produce a smelly odour. To defend themselves from predators, they use their knife-like tusks.

- Scorpions often bury themselves in sand to avoid the hot sun. The scorpion's hard, outer shell helps to keep moisture inside its body.

- Stiff tufts of hair protect the bottoms of a kit fox's feet from the hot desert ground.

Comprehension questions

1. Describe how the passing of time is shown throughout this book.

2. Name three diurnal predators in the Sonoran Desert, and their prey. Then name three nocturnal predators and their prey.

Glossary

adapt change to fit into a new or different environment

burrow tunnel or hole in the ground made or used by an animal for shelter

cactus pad flat, paddle-shaped stem of certain cacti, such as the prickly pear

climate average weather of a place throughout the year

diurnal active during the day

habitat natural home or environment of an animal, plant or other living thing

horizon line where the sky and the land or sea appear to meet

inject put into

nectar sweet liquid found in many flowers

nocturnal active at night

predator animal that hunts other animals

prey animal hunted by another animal

talon long, sharp claw of a bird

venomous full of venom; a poison injected into a victim by biting or stinging

vibrate move quickly from side to side with small movements

Read more

Desert Food Chains (Food Chains and Webs), Angela Royston (Raintree, 2014)

Exploring Deserts (Exploring Habitats), Anita Ganeri (Raintree, 2014)

Living and Non-Living in the Desert (Is It Living or Non-living?), Rebecca Rissman (Raintree, 2014)

Index

Websites

www.ucmp.berkeley.edu/glossary/gloss5/biome/deserts.html

Learn more about the desert biome and understand how desert biomes are classified.

www.livescience.com/23140-sahara-desert.html

Explore the extremes of the Sahara desert on this website and see some fascinating video clips.

Special thanks to our advisers for their expertise, research and advice:

Cecil R. Schwalbe, PhD, Wildlife and Fisheries Program
University of Arizona, Tucson

Terry Flaherty, PhD, Professor of English
Minnesota State University, Mankato

Raintree is an imprint of Capstone Global Library Limited, a company incorporated in England and Wales having its registered office at 7 Pilgrim Street, London, EC4V 6LB – Registered company number: 6695582

www.raintree.co.uk
myorders@raintree.co.uk

Editorial credits:
Jill Kalz, editor; Lori Bye, designer; Nathan Gassman, art director; Kathy McColley, production specialist

ISBN 978 1 4062 9418 7
18 17 16 15 14
10 9 8 7 6 5 4 3 2 1

British Library Cataloguing in Publication Data
A full catalogue record for this book is available from the British Library.

The illustrations in this book were created with cut paper.
Design Elements: Shutterstock/Alfondo de Tomas (map),
    Alvaro Cabrera Jimenez

All the Internet addresses (URLs) given in this book were valid at the time of going to press. However, due to the dynamic nature of the Internet, some addresses may have changed, or sites may have changed or ceased to exist since publication. While the author and publisher regret any inconvenience this may cause readers, no responsibility for any such changes can be accepted by either the author or the publisher.

Look out for all the books in the series:

A Day and Night in the Amazon Rainforest

A Day and Night in the Sonoran Desert

Printed in China.   3656